UP and DOWN

Written by Elaine Marie Larson

Illustrated by Wayne Andreason

Jump up!

You come down with a *thud*.

Throw your ball up!

It falls down with a *thump*.

Things that go up
come back down.
This is called gravity.
You cannot see, taste,
hear, or smell it.
But you can feel it.

Run down a hill.

It is easy.

Gravity pulls you to the bottom.

Run up a hill.

It is hard.

You and gravity play tug-of-war.

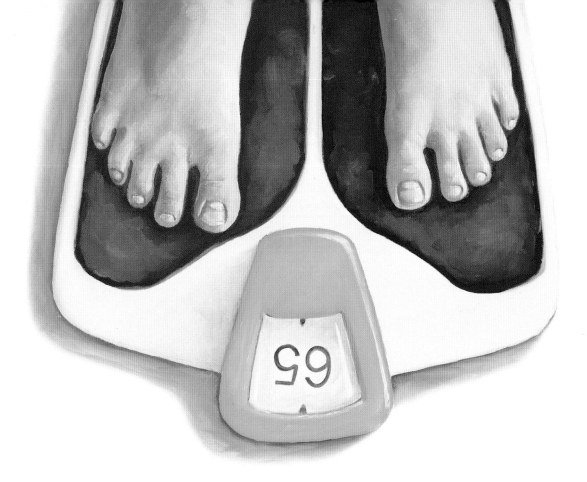

Gravity pulls down on you.

A scale shows how hard it pulls.

Gravity is your friend.

It holds your bike on the ground.

It keeps you on your bike.

It keeps your feet on the petals.

Pretend gravity went away.
Could you ride your bike?
Could you play catch?

Gravity never goes away.

It never stops working.

Gravity never needs sleep.

But when you are sleepy, lie down.

Gravity will keep you in bed

until you get up.